RENEWABLE ENERGY SOURCES

WIND, SOLAR AND HYDRO ENERGY EDITION

ENVIRONMENT BOOKS FOR KIDS

Children's Environment Books

In this book, we're going to talk about three important renewable energy sources, wind, solar, and hydroelectric power. So, let's get right to it!

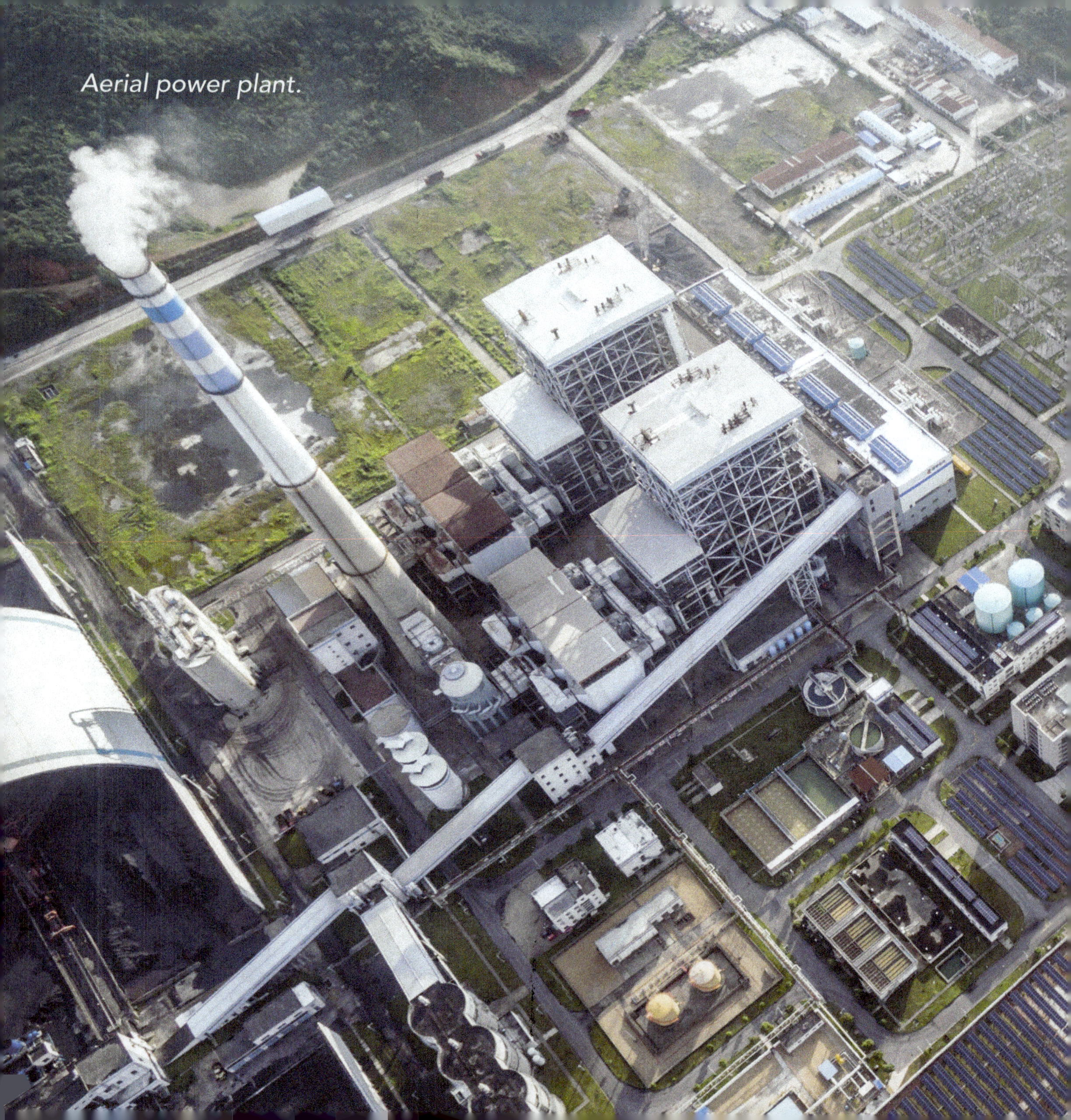

Aerial power plant.

WHAT'S THE DIFFERENCE BETWEEN NON-RENEWABLE AND RENEWABLE ENERGY SOURCES?

Human beings need energy to power homes, manufacturing facilities, and transportation, and as our population grows we need more and more energy. There are two types of energy sources: non-renewable and renewable. Fossil fuels, such as coal and petroleum, are examples of non-renewable energy sources. These fuels were formed by natural processes deep in the Earth over hundreds of millions of years, so once these resources are used up, we won't have them available.

The other issue with fossil fuels is that when they are burned they give out carbon dioxide. Our atmosphere has natural carbon dioxide, but when too much excess carbon dioxide gets into the air it causes toxic pollution. It also causes something called *"The Greenhouse Effect."* The excess CO_2 starts increasing the temperature worldwide, causing global warming.

Oil and Gas Pump in the Mountains.

In the 1800s, the amount of carbon dioxide in the atmosphere was 280 parts per million. Today it has increased by about 40% and is 400 parts per million. Most scientists believe that if the resulting increase in temperature continues it will have disastrous consequences for our planet. Global warming will have the following effects:

- A rise in the level of our oceans, as ice from the poles melts

- An increase in the temperature of air and water worldwide

- Extreme weather events, such as killer hurricanes and massive floods

- A huge change in animal and plant life as an adjustment to the shift in temperature

It's not clear at this point whether the effects of global warming can be reversed. Scientists all over the world have been pushing for countries to change the sources of energy they use. This has led to new inventions in the field of renewable energy sources. Renewable energy is energy that will always be available for us to harness and use.

Solar panel and wind power.

CHARACTERISTICS OF RENEWABLE ENERGY

There are three basic characteristics of renewable energy.

- Renewable energy sources don't pollute the water, land, or air.

- They are *"Carbon Neutral,"* which means that they don't give off carbon compounds like CO_2 in the process of being used.

- They can't run out because the source that creates them is unlimited, like the sun for solar power and the wind for wind power.

P ower from the wind, power from the sun, and power from moving water are three types of renewable energy sources. At the current time, only 10% of the energy in the United States is generated from renewable sources. However, these industries are poised for growth, which means that they will be providing much more of the energy needed in the US and worldwide in the future.

Wind Turbines At The Base Of A Foothill.

POWER FROM
THE WIND

When the sun warms the Earth, not all places are warmed to the same temperature. The surface of the land heats up faster than water surfaces do. Warm air always rises. As the warm air starts to expand and then rises in the atmosphere, cooler air moves into the space where the warm air used to be.

This moving of warmer air and cooler air creates wind. At night, the opposite happens. Once the sun goes down, the wind reverses, since the air over land gets cooler more quickly than it does over water.

Clean energy concept.

HOW DO WIND TURBINES WORK?

There are two types of wind turbines. One has horizontal blades and the other has vertical blades. Most of the turbines in use today are horizontal-blade turbines because they work better than the vertical type.

Wind Turbine Construction.

HORIZONTAL-BLADE WIND TURBINES

A horizontal-blade turbine has three blades that spin high in the air. The blades look like airplane propellers. The length of the three blades on this type of turbine is directly related to how much electricity it can create. The longer the blades are, the more power they can generate. The smallest wind turbines might only have a capacity of 10 kilowatts of power, but large ones can create up to 8,000 kilowatts. In locations where there is adequate wind, larger turbines are positioned in what is called a *"Wind Farm."*

Wind Turbine in Denmark.

M any of these larger turbines are the same
height as a building with 20 stories. Their
blades can be over 100 feet long.

   The wind's movement creates kinetic energy.
As the wind moves over the turbine's blades it
creates lift on them and this causes them to turn.
The blades connect to a shaft. This drive shaft
spins a motor that generates electrical power.

Brightly lit windmill against dramatic clouds.

Wind turbines work in the exact opposite way to the way a fan works. A fan uses electricity to create wind to cool you down. A wind turbine uses wind to create electricity.

In 2015, about 5% of all the electricity in the United States was generated by the power of the wind. Wind power is one of the fastest growing of the renewable energy sources and in the next 10 years it will create lots of new jobs.

Wind Turbines.

DISADVANTAGES OF WIND POWER

Some people don't like the way wind farms look over the landscape or the sound they make. Sometimes birds or bats are killed when they fly into the wind turbines and wind energy companies are researching how this problem can be solved.

Windmills with container ship in a harbor.

Photovoltaic power plant.

POWER FROM THE SUN

The sun is really the Earth's main source of energy. Solar power is unlimited and doesn't create any pollution. Power from the sun that we can harness is used for heating and for electricity.

SOLAR THERMAL ENERGY SYSTEMS

These technologies are used to generate heat from the rays of the sun. A pump moves cold water that's been stored in a tank through pipes in some type of solar collector or panel. These collectors are located on rooftops or other places where they can get the most sun exposure. The water is then heated up by the sun and then goes back to the tank. This type of thermal energy is used to heat water for hot water tanks, to heat swimming pools, or to heat water or air for warming up rooms in a building during the winter.

Solar panels.

SOLAR PHOTOVOLTAIC SYSTEMS

These technologies are used to generate electrical power from the rays of the sun. Scientists at Bell Laboratories created the first photovoltaic cell, called PV cell for short, in 1954. You might have a calculator or a wristwatch whose power comes from a PV cell. Many of the solar panels that are used on the rooftops of houses are arrays of PV cells.

Photovoltaic Cells.

Unlike solar thermal systems that convert the sun's rays to usable heat, PV cells are designed to convert the energy from the sun into electrical energy. Putting these types of solar cells on a house is expensive, but the house's utility bills are sometimes zeroed out or the household may even have extra electricity that they can sell back to the city.

Solar Power Plant.

HOW DO PV CELLS WORK?

The process of how photovoltaic cells work is easy to remember if you think of how the word is made up of "photons," the particles that light is composed of and "voltage," the way electricity is measured. Hot, powerful sunlight beams down on the solar PV cell. The photons begin to react with the layers of crystal silicon in the cell.

Row of solar panels on roof.

The reaction causes the electrons in the silicon atoms to start moving. The bottom layer of crystals has been created so it needs those loose electrons to become stable. The electrons start moving around from the top of the cell to the bottom of the cell. This movement is what causes the generation of electricity.

DISADVANTAGES OF SOLAR POWER

There are several disadvantages to solar power. One problem is that the sun may be as available on some days versus others depending on the weather. Another problem is that photovoltaic cells are expensive and it takes a lot of them to create a large amount of electrical power.

Electricity from hydropower plants.

POWER FROM MOVING WATER

Electricity generated by moving water, called hydro energy, accounts for about ¼ of all the renewable energy that is used in the United States. The kinetic energy from moving water in dams or waterfalls can be harnessed. As the water travels through pipes at a very high speed, it spins generator shafts. In turn, these shafts create electricity.

DISADVANTAGES OF HYDROELECTRIC POWER

Building hydroelectric power plants requires a lot of money. However, once built, they don't require a great many workers or maintenance. There are a limited number of natural geographic areas that are suitable for power plants.

Hydro power plant.

Holding water in dams and changing the natural water flow does have some environmental consequences for the fish that are native to an area. Roads need to be constructed and power lines need to be put in to support the plants as well, which has an affect on the environment.

Awesome! Now you know more about the different types of renewable energy sources. You can find more Environment books from Baby Professor by searching the website of your favorite book retailer.

Visit
BABY PROFESSOR
EDUCATION KIDS
www.BabyProfessorBooks.com
to download Free Baby Professor eBooks
and view our catalog of new and exciting
Children's Books